WELCOME TO MY COUNTRY

Welcome to
UGANDA

Gareth Stevens Publishing
A WORLD ALMANAC EDUCATION GROUP COMPANY

Written by
GRACE PUNDYK

Edited by
MELVIN NEO

Edited in USA by
JENETTE DONOVAN GUNTLY

Designed by
GEOSLYN LIM

Picture research by
SUSAN JANE MANUEL
THOMAS KHOO

First published in North America in 2005 by
Gareth Stevens Publishing
A World Almanac Education Group Company
330 West Olive Street, Suite 100
Milwaukee, Wisconsin 53212 USA

Please visit our web site at
www.garethstevens.com
For a free color catalog describing
Gareth Stevens Publishing's list of high-quality
books and multimedia programs,
call 1-800-542-2595 (USA) or
1-800-387-3178 (Canada).
Gareth Stevens Publishing's fax: (414) 332-3567.

© **MARSHALL CAVENDISH INTERNATIONAL (ASIA)**
PRIVATE LIMITED 2005
Originated and designed by
Times Editions Marshall Cavendish
An imprint of Marshall Cavendish International (Asia) Pte Ltd
A member of Times Publishing Limited
Times Centre, 1 New Industrial Road
Singapore 536196
http://www.marshallcavendish.com/genref

Library of Congress Cataloging-in-Publication Data
Pundyk, Grace.
Welcome to Uganda / by Grace Pundyk.
p. cm. — (Welcome to my country)
Includes bibliographical references and index.
ISBN 0-8368-3130-6 (lib. bdg.)
1. Uganda — Juvenile literature. I. Title. II. Series.
DT433.222.P86   2005
967.61—dc22   2004056648

Printed in Singapore

1 2 3 4 5 6 7 8 9 09 08 07 06 05

PICTURE CREDITS
ANA Photo and Press Agency: 1, 2, 17,
    23, 24, 25
Art Directors & TRIP Photo Library: 3
    (center), 4, 5, 20, 22 (both), 28, 35
Camera Press Ltd: 39
Camerapix: cover, 3 (top), 14, 15 (all),
    27, 30, 33, 36, 37, 40, 41, 45
Getty Images/Hulton Archive: 12
Chris van Houts: 29 (left)
Images of Africa Photobank: 9, 16, 26
Paul Joynson-Hicks/Lauré
    Communications: 6, 7, 8, 18, 43
Jason Lauré/Lauré Communications: 32
Lonely Planet Images: 38
North Wind Picture Archives: 10, 11
Mark Olencki: 29 (right)
Robert Pateman: 19, 21, 31, 34
Topham Picturepoint: 13
Alison Wright: 3 (bottom)

Digital Scanning by Superskill Graphics Pte Ltd

Contents

Words that appear in the glossary are printed in **boldface** type the first time they occur in the text.

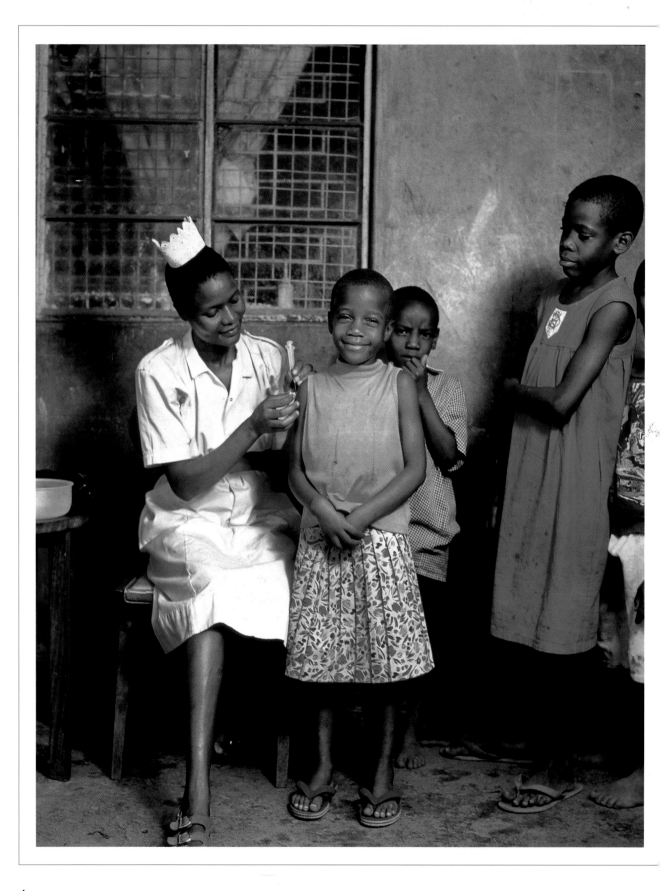

Welcome to Uganda!

Uganda is a beautiful country in East Africa. It has many green fields and high mountains. The country also has many animals, including elephants and lions. For years, the country suffered under Idi Amin's harsh rule. Today, Uganda is trying to recover from a bad economy and poor health-care system. Let's visit Uganda and meet its people!

Opposite: These children are getting their shots. Health care in Uganda has improved, but many people still do not have proper care.

Below: Uganda's education system was changed in the mid-1990s. After that, the number of children attending school doubled.

The Flag of Uganda

Uganda's flag is made up of six black, yellow, and red bands. Black stands for the Ugandans. Yellow stands for sunshine. Red stands for the **brotherhood** of Ugandans. The crested crane in the center is Uganda's national symbol.

The Land

Uganda is surrounded by five countries. Sudan is to the north. Kenya is to the east. Tanzania is to the south. Rwanda to the southwest, and the Democratic Republic of the Congo is to the west. Uganda has an area of 91,111 square miles (236,040 square kilometers). The center of the country is mostly flat. Mountains and valleys surround it. Margherita Peak in the Ruwenzori Range is the highest point in Uganda. It is 16,795 feet (5,119 meters) high.

Below: Margherita Peak is located in the southwest of the country. Because it is so high, the peak is usually covered with snow and ice. Clouds often hide the peak from view.

Left: The Nile is described as the "father of African rivers." It begins in Uganda, near the city of Jinja.

Rivers and Lakes

Uganda has several large rivers and lakes. The Victoria Nile is one of the country's main rivers. It starts in Lake Victoria, which is Africa's largest lake. The Victoria Nile ends at Lake Albert. It flows out the other side of the lake as the Albert Nile. The Victoria Nile and Albert Nile form the beginnings of the Nile River, which is the longest river in the world. The Nile flows across the lands of northeastern Africa for about 4,132 miles (6,648 km). At its end, it empties into the Mediterranean Sea.

Climate

Uganda is located near the **equator**. Because it is mostly on a high **plateau**, Uganda has a dryer and cooler climate than most lands near the equator. The country's lakes, cool mountain breezes, and clouds make it dryer and cooler, too. Uganda has three climate regions. The Northern Savanna, or grasslands, is dry and warm. The Lake Region, near Lake Victoria, is damp and warm. The Southern Highlands are dry and cool.

Below: Uganda gets lots of rain, so the country is covered in many kinds of lush, green plants and trees. Uganda is warm enough for them to grow most of the year.

Left: The African Cape Buffalo is one of the many animal species found in the Queen Elizabeth National Park.

Plants and Animals

Uganda has many kinds of plants. Some forests grew in the country. Many of the trees, including mahogany, nongo, and muzizi trees, have been cut down. They are in danger because of logging.

Uganda has many kinds of animals, including zebras, elephants, giraffes, antelopes, hippopotamuses, and rare mountain gorillas. Large cats, such as lions and leopards, now live mainly in Uganda's national parks and **reserves**. Over a thousand kinds of birds live in Uganda, including flamingos, storks, cranes, doves, and pelicans.

History

Bantu-speaking people arrived in what is now Uganda between 500 B.C. and A.D. 1000. In the 1300s, they formed kingdoms that later became the states of Bunyoro, Buganda, and Ankole. By the 1800s, Bunyoro had become the largest state, but Buganda later grew larger.

Left: This picture is of Mutesa I (*left, seated*). He was the *kabaka* (KAH-bah-kah), or ruler, of Buganda. During his rule, trade with foreign countries increased. During that time, religions that were not **native** to Buganda began to arrive, including the Islamic religion and Christianity.

In 1884, Mwanga became kabaka of Buganda. He was taken out of power in 1888 after trying to make **missionaries** leave Buganda. The Protestants, Roman Catholics, and followers of Islam then fought for control. The Protestants and Catholics put Mwanga back in power in 1889. He ruled even after Britain took control in 1890. In 1894, Buganda was made a British **protectorate**. By 1914, the region was known as the Uganda protectorate. It had set boundaries and a central government.

British Rule

In the 1900s, the British helped build many railroad tracks in Uganda. They also improved farming. Even though the changes helped, Uganda's economy grew most after South Asian businesses arrived. In the 1920s and 1930s, Britain began to reduce the control Buganda's rulers had. In 1953, Kabaka Mutesa II was forced out of the country. In 1955, he returned as ruler, but relations with British-controlled Uganda were tense.

Left:
Kabaka Mutesa II inspects the guard of honor as part of his birthday celebrations on November 1, 1951.

Left: Milton Obote (*second from right*) swears allegiance to Queen Elizabeth II of Great Britain. He became Uganda's first prime minister in 1962. When Idi Amin took control in 1971, Obote had to flee the country.

From Independence to Amin

By the 1960s, many Ugandans wanted freedom from Britain. On October 9, 1962, Uganda became **independent**, and Buganda and four other kingdoms became states. Each state had a right to self-govern. Milton Obote became the prime minister. In 1963, the kabaka of Buganda, Mutesa II, became president. Supporters of Obote and of Mutesa II fought for control. In 1966, Obote made laws that took away Buganda's right to self-govern. He sent in troops led by Colonel Idi Amin. Amin took over and forced Mutesa II to flee to Britain. In 1971, Amin forced Obote out of power.

The Rule of Amin

Uganda suffered under the harsh rule of Idi Amin. He forced South Asians who owned businesses to leave. After that, the economy crashed. Between 100,000 and 300,000 Ugandans were murdered during his rule. In April 1979, he was taken out of power. Milton Obote came back in 1980 and became president. In 1985, he was taken out of power again. General Tito Okello took over. In 1986, Yoweri Museveni took control.

Left: In the past and today, some **rebel** groups in Uganda have used children as soldiers. Many other nations have spoken out against the practice.

Apollo Milton Obote (1924–)

Apollo Milton Obote led Uganda to independence in 1962. He served as prime minister from 1962 to 1966. He became president in 1966 and again in 1980. In 1985, he was forced to flee the country. He now lives in Zambia.

Apollo Milton Obote

Yoweri Kaguta Museveni (1944–)

Yoweri Kaguta Museveni formed the Front for National **Salvation** in 1971. The group overthrew Amin in 1979. Since 1986, as Uganda's president, he has increased respect for human rights and has also improved the economy.

Yoweri Kaguta Museveni

Dr. Wandira Specioza Kazibwe (1955–)

Dr. Wandira Specioza Kazibwe became vice president of Uganda in 1994. She was the first woman in all of Africa to hold such a high government position. She is known for her work to improve human rights and rights for women.

Dr. Wandira Specioza Kazibwe

Government and the Economy

Uganda's government consists of three branches. The executive branch runs the government and makes rules for it. It is led by the president, who picks a prime minister and a cabinet, which is a group of advisors. The judicial branch is made up of the Court of Appeal and the High Court. The **legislative** branch is made up of the National Assembly.

Below: The National Assembly is a 305-member **parliament**. The assembly holds its meetings in the parliament building (*below*) in Kampala, which is the capital city of Uganda.

All Ugandans over age eighteen can vote. The National Assembly has 214 elected members. The rest of the seats are given to government advisors, the military, and members who represent disabled people, workers, and youths.

Uganda has ten **provinces**, which are headed by governors chosen by the president. Each province is then divided into regions called districts. Each of the fifty-six districts must have one female member in the National Assembly.

Above: A soldier looks out from a Ugandan tank. When Ugandan boys turn fifteen, they can join the military. Men are able to serve in Uganda's military until they are forty-nine years old.

The Economy

Most Ugandans work in farming. Some crops in the country are grown mainly to sell to other countries, including tea, coffee, cotton, sugarcane, and flowers. In 2000, Germany, the Netherlands, and the United States bought most of these products. Most crops are grown to feed Ugandans, however, including peppers, cabbages, tomatoes, carrots, soybeans, corn, and **plantains**. Many farmers also produce milk, cheese, beef, poultry, and mutton, which is the meat of sheep.

Below: Most people in Uganda still use **traditional** methods of farming, such as using their hands instead of machines to sort large piles of coffee beans.

Left: This large sign is advertising a kind of bottled beer that is made in Uganda. Besides beer, a few other products are made in Uganda, including matches, soap, and shoes.

Some of Uganda's other industries relate to farming, including processing the coffee, tea, and cotton produced.

Tourism is also an important industry in Uganda. Under the rule of Idi Amin, tourism stopped. After he left, tourism began to grow again. Today, tourists come to visit Uganda's national parks and see its many animals. Fighting in countries around Uganda has kept many tourists away, however.

Uganda is still recovering from years of a very bad economy. Today, a great many Ugandans are still very poor.

People and Lifestyle

Uganda's People

Many people in Uganda are young. In 2003, about half of all Ugandans were under age fourteen. More than eighteen different **ethnic** groups live in Uganda. The largest group is the Baganda, or "Ganda people." Other large groups in the country include the Ankole, Basoga, and Iteso. Smaller groups include the Bakiga, Lango, and Rwanda. A few of the people in Uganda are Europeans, Jews, Arabs, or South Asians.

Left: The people living in this village, in the northeastern part of Uganda, are from the Karamojong ethnic group.

Rural and Urban Life

Most Ugandans live in the countryside and most do some farming. Many of the country's wealthier farmers live in the north. They can afford to raise cattle. In central, eastern, and southern Uganda, most **rural** homes have large pieces of land, which are used to grow crops or keep animals such as goats.

Most of Uganda's **urban** areas are in the south. Many Ugandans move to the cities to find work but cannot. Many of them end up living on the streets.

Above: This street is in Jinja, a city in southern Uganda. Since the 1990s, the number of children living on Uganda's streets has gone up.

Family

Families are very important in Uganda. It is common in rural areas for many family members to live in the same house, including grandparents, parents, children, aunts, uncles, and cousins. Traditionally, men are the heads of their households. In rural areas, women are always expected to obey their husbands. The laws do not help wives if their husbands leave or die. Some Ugandan women suffer violence in their homes.

Above: In Uganda, some unmarried women are finding jobs outside their homes. Traditional Ugandans do not approve, however. They feel women should stay home.

Left: This family lives in Masaka. In a traditional Ugandan family, the father usually holds a job outside the home or is a farmer. The mother is usually in charge of the home and the children.

Health care in Uganda

In 2003, only about half of Ugandans had access to medical centers. A lack of medicines and clean water makes the problems worse. Many Ugandans suffer from diseases, such as chicken pox and measles, that are easily cured in countries with good health care.

Out of every thousand babies born in Uganda, ninety babies die. Men live an average of forty-three years. Women live an average of forty-five years.

Above: These two nurses are helping patients at Saint Mary's Hospital in the district of Gulu. Uganda's doctors and nurses have worked hard to slow the spread of many serious diseases, including HIV/AIDS.

Education

Universal Primary Education (UPE) was introduced by President Yoweri Museveni in 1997. UPE provides free education for up to four children in every family. If a family includes girls and boys, two of the students must be girls. Disabled children who apply are given top priority. By 1999, the number of students between ages six and fifteen who attended school rose from about 2.5 million to 6.5 million. Many more of the students finished school as well.

Below: Students from Kaapi Primary School surround Joseph Okungu, who is the school's director. Primary school is the first level of school in Uganda. Students start school at age six and attend for seven years.

After primary school, students go on to lower secondary school, which lasts four years. After they complete lower secondary school, students can choose to attend upper secondary school, which lasts two years, or a technical school, which lasts up to three years. In upper secondary school, students prepare to attend a university. Technical school prepares students for a profession.

Religion

Although there is no official religion in Uganda, most Ugandans are Christians. Most Christians in Uganda are Roman Catholic or Protestant. Small groups of Presbyterians, Seventh Day Adventists, and Baptists live in the country as well.

Christianity in Uganda dates back to the 1800s, when Protestant and Roman Catholic missionaries arrived. From the start, the groups have not gotten along. They have fought for power in Uganda and also have fought over who could win more **converts**. Today, the groups get along better with people from other religions than they do with each other.

Left: Kampala has many grand Roman Catholic cathedrals, such as the Rubaga and Saint Peter's cathedrals. Most of the cathedrals have fancy decorations on the outside.

Islam and Traditional Religions

Some Ugandans are followers of Islam and are called Muslims. Islam is said to have come to Uganda in the 1800s from North African nations and from traders arriving from East Africa's coast.

Some Ugandans believe in traditional African religions. Most believers pray to **ancestral** spirits and make **sacrifices** to ask for protection in their daily lives. The religions are known for the belief that older people, both living and dead, are powerful. Some Ugandans believe that their living elders can curse family members with illness or bad luck.

Above: The Kibuli Mosque in Kampala opened in 1951. A mosque is a house of worship for Muslims. Both Sunni and Shi'ite Muslims live in Uganda. The two groups believe in slightly different versions of Islam.

Language

English is Uganda's official language. It is used in government and in schools. English is also used in newspapers and radio programs. Only about one million Ugandans speak English well, though. Most people speak one of forty native languages. Many Ugandans speak the Ganda, or Luganda, language. Other native languages in the country include Chiga, Nyankore, Soga, Acholi, Teso, Masaba, Aringa, Lango, and Rwanda. Two native languages have died out.

Left: In addition to English and native languages, many Ugandans also speak Swahili. The language allows Ugandans to trade and to do business with people from neighboring nations such as Ethiopia, Kenya, Tanzania, and Sudan.

Literature

Today, Uganda has a growing number of authors who are famous around the world. Most Ugandan authors began to publish their works after the country became independent in 1962. One of Uganda's most-loved authors is Okot P'Bitek (1931–1982). He wrote many works, including *Lak Tar* (1953) and *Horn of My Love* (1974). Some foreign authors, such as Giles Foden, have lived in Uganda and have written about the country. His recent book, *The Last King of Scotland* (1998), won many awards.

Arts

Ugandan Crafts

Ugandan crafts include cloth making, pottery, and basketry. Cloth in Uganda used to be made from animal skins or tree bark. Many Ugandans now make cotton cloth. It often has fancy sewing or printed designs. Clay pots are often made to store drinks and food. Metal pots are used for cooking. Baskets are usually made of banana **fibers**. Some baskets are used by farmers to sift dirt from coffee beans or grains.

Left: Uganda's colorful baskets are woven by hand and come in many shapes and sizes. Baskets are so much a part of life in Uganda that almost every bride will receive at least one among her wedding gifts.

Left: The Kasubi Tombs are located in Kampala. The building is over 120 years old. When it was first built, the structure was meant to be a palace for Baganda kabakas. Two years later, the building was made into a burial place for members of the royal family.

Architecture

Architecture in Uganda's rural areas is mostly made up of mud huts that have **thatched** roofs. Paintings often cover both the inside and outside of the huts. Some wealthy rural families can afford houses built from bricks and cement. Most homes in Jinja, Uganda's second-largest city, were built by South Asians. The houses have large front rooms and many bedrooms. When Idi Amin took control, he made all South Asians leave. Ugandan African families then moved into the homes. Most Ugandans in the **suburbs** live in apartment buildings.

Music

Most Ugandans love listening to music. In cities, many Ugandans go to bars or discos to hear the latest music. Most Ugandans enjoy listening to traditional music, however, especially when it is played along with traditional dances. Xylophones are the key instruments played in traditional music. One kind, the *amadinda* (AH-mah-din-dah), takes two people to play. It has fifteen or more keys. The *akadinda* (AH-kah-din-dah) has up to twenty keys. A twenty-key akadinda is played by four people.

Left: A group of Ugandan musicians performs traditional music in Kampala. Some of the many instruments played in traditional music include shakers, drums, rattles, fiddles, and flutes.

Dance

Each of Uganda's regions and ethnic groups has its own traditional dances. In the south, most dances involve fast waist movements. In the north, dances are mostly made up of foot, arm, and neck movements. In the southwest and northeast, dances often involve leaping and stomping. Many traditional dances honor special occasions. The Baganda, for instance, have dances for births and weddings and to entertain the kabaka.

Above: These dancers are from the Ndere Troupe. This dance group is well known both in Uganda and around the world for its talented dancers.

Leisure

Most Ugandans live in rural areas. They usually have little leisure time because they must care for their crops and farm animals. Children also have little leisure time. After school, they must do chores, such as cleaning and fetching water. If people have leisure time, they often like to sing and dance or watch other people sing and dance. In cities, many people watch music or theater performances.

Below: These Ugandans are playing *Omweso* (OM-wee-soh), a favorite board game in Uganda. There are thirty-two holes on the board and the game uses sixty-four seeds. The aim of the game is to capture as many of the other player's seeds as possible.

The Tradition of Storytelling

In Uganda, storytelling is so popular
that it has become part of the school
program. During storytelling sessions,
students tell stories they learned from
family members. In cities, where many
children no longer tell stories on their
own, storytelling in school helps keep
very old Ugandan folktales alive. Two
favorite stories explain why the sun
rises and how zebras got their stripes.

Above: Ugandan
storytellers must
sometimes sing
a few songs while
telling a story. It is
through storytelling
that many Ugandan
folk songs grew.

Sports

Ugandans play many sports, including cricket, rugby, tennis, **squash**, boxing, and wrestling. Cricket is a game that is somewhat similar to baseball. It was brought to Uganda by the British. Now, the country is home to talented cricket players such as Kenneth Kamyuka and Frank Nsubuga. Ugandans also enjoy track and field events, especially events involving running. Davis Kamoga won a bronze medal in the 400-meter track race in the 1996 Olympic Games.

Below: This golf course is in Jinja. Few Ugandans can afford to play golf because the sport requires expensive equipment and a club membership.

36

Soccer

Soccer is probably the best-loved sport in Uganda. Often, groups of children can be seen playing soccer in fields all over the country. Only certain schools have soccer teams in Uganda. If young players want to become professionals, they must attend a school with a soccer team. Players can then work their way up to national or international levels. Uganda's oldest team, the Express FC or "Red Eagles," was founded in 1957.

Above: Ugandans love playing and watching soccer. Medi Bonseu is a well-known soccer player in Uganda. He played on the national team and is now chairman of the Ugandan Players Association (UPA).

Religious Holidays

Most religious holidays in Uganda are Christian or Muslim. Many Christian Ugandans celebrate Christmas, during which they usually attend church, spend time with family, and visit with friends. Some Ugandans also celebrate holidays such as Easter and Good Friday. *Eid al-Fitr* (EED AHL-fitr) is the most widely celebrated Muslim festival. It is held to celebrate the end of the Islamic holy month of **Ramadan**.

Left: John Baptist Kaggwa (*center, wearing hat*) is the Catholic bishop of Masaka. Catholics around Uganda celebrate when he comes to town.

National Holidays and Festivals

Uganda's national holidays include International Women's Day (March 8), National Heroes' Day (June 9), and Independence Day (October 9). Each year, the Uganda Development Theatre Association (UDTA) holds a theater festival. Out of nine hundred groups, thirty-six groups are chosen to perform. The performances help keep traditional Ugandan culture alive. Also, new and different forms of theater are shown.

Left: Large groups of Ugandans and foreigners living in Uganda attend the Royal Ascot Goat Races. The races are held in Entebbe every September.

Food

Meals in Uganda are usually heavy and filling. Foods such as *matooke* (mah-TOE-kee) and *ugali* (oo-GAH-lee) are served with almost all meals. Matooke is mashed plantains. Ugali is a type of corn bread. Other main foods include yams, potatoes, or **cassavas**. Meats and boiled vegetables are often served with these main foods. Stews with meat and sauces made from beans or peanuts are often served with main dishes as well. Most dishes are flavored only with salt.

Left:
These Ugandans are filling bowls with corn. Corn is used to make many foods in the country. It is used fresh, dried, or ground up in different ways.

Left: This woman is selling different kinds of smoked fish and meats. Small food stalls such as this one are a common sight in Uganda.

Most Ugandans love to eat meat, especially goat and chicken. Fish such as Nile perch and tilapia are popular as well. Common dishes include roasts, meat stews, and smoked meat and fish. Grilled or fried lamb chops and chicken are favorites, too. *Luwombo* (lu-WOM-boh) is a dish made of goat, beef, pork, or chicken in a rich tomato sauce. It is wrapped in banana leaves and steamed.

Some Ugandans drink *pombe* (POM-bee), or banana beer. Some people also drink *waragi* (WAH-rah-gee), a drink made from a grain called millet.

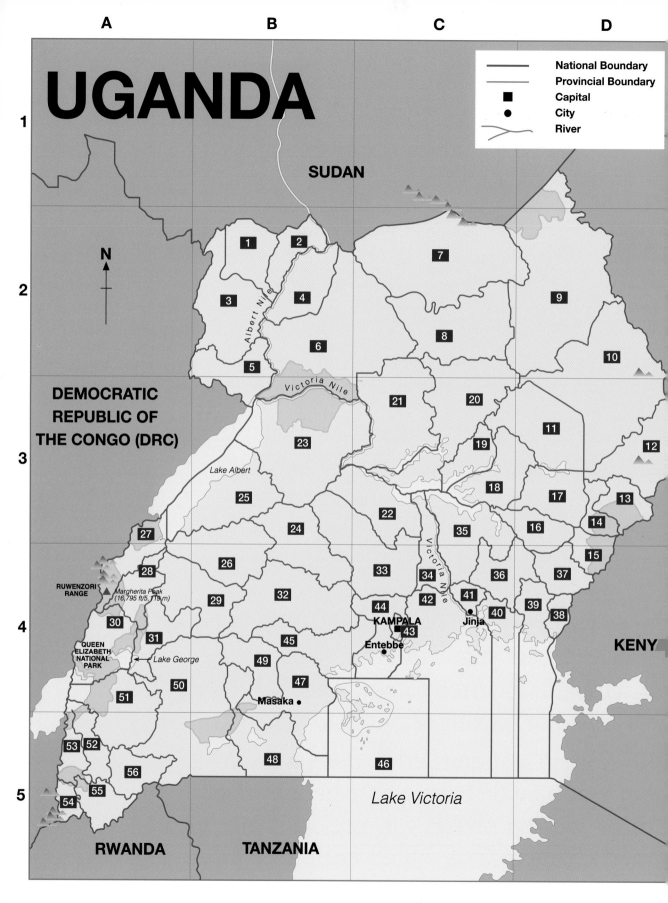

UGANDA

N

SUDAN

DEMOCRATIC
REPUBLIC OF
THE CONGO (DRC)

Albert Nile

Victoria Nile

Lake Albert

RUWENZORI
RANGE

Margherita Peak
(16,795 ft/5,119 m)

QUEEN
ELIZABETH
NATIONAL
PARK

Lake George

KAMPALA

Entebbe

Jinja

Victoria Nile

Masaka

KENY

Lake Victoria

RWANDA

TANZANIA

	National Boundary
	Provincial Boundary
■	Capital
●	City
	River

42

DISTRICTS

1 Yumbe
2 Moyo
3 Arua
4 Adjumani
5 Nebbi
6 Gulu
7 Kitgum
8 Pader
9 Kotido
10 Moroto
11 Katakwi
12 Nakapiripirit
13 Kapchorwa
14 Sironko
15 Mbale
16 Pallisa
17 Kumi
18 Soroti
19 Kaberamaido
20 Lira
21 Apac
22 Nakasongola
23 Masindi
24 Kiboga
25 Hoima
26 Kibale
27 Bundibugyo
28 Kabarole
29 Kyenjojo
30 Kasese
31 Kamwenge
32 Mubende
33 Luwero
34 Kayunga
35 Kamuli
36 Iganga
37 Tororo
38 Busia
39 Bugiri
40 Mayuge
41 Jinja
42 Mukono
43 Kampala
44 Wakiso
45 Mpigi
46 Kalangala
47 Masaka
48 Rakai
49 Sembabule
50 Mbarara
51 Bushenyi
52 Rukungiri
53 Kanungu
54 Kisoro
55 Kabale
56 Ntungamo

Above: This school on Bwama Island in Lake Bunyoni teaches students to weave.

Albert Nile B2–B3

Democratic Republic
  of the Congo
  (DRC) A1–A5

Entebbe C4

Jinja C4

Kampala C4
Kenya D1–D5

Lake Albert A3–B3
Lake Victoria B4–D5

Margherita Peak A4
Masaka B4

Queen Elizabeth
  National Park
  A4–A5

Ruwenzori
  Range A4
Rwanda A5–B5

Sudan A1–D1

Tanzania A5–D5

Victoria Nile B3–C4

Quick Facts

Official Name	Republic of Uganda
Capital	Kampala
Official Language	English
Land Area	91,111 square miles (236,040 square kilometers)
Districts	Adjumani, Apac, Arua, Bugiri, Bundibugyo, Bushenyi, Busia, Gulu, Hoima, Iganga, Jinja, Kabale, Kabarole, Kaberamaido, Kalangala, Kampala, Kamuli, Kamwenge, Kanungu, Kapchorwa, Kasese, Katakwi, Kayunga, Kibale, Kiboga, Kisoro, Kitgum, Kotido, Kumi, Kyenjojo, Lira, Luwero, Masaka, Masindi, Mayuge, Mbale, Mbarara, Moroto, Moyo, Mpigi, Mubende, Mukono, Nakapiripirit, Nakasongola, Nebbi, Ntungamo, Pader, Pallisa, Rakai, Rukungiri, Sembabule, Sironko, Soroti, Tororo, Wakiso, Yumbe
Highest Point	Margherita Peak 16,795 feet (5,119 m)
Major Rivers	Victoria Nile, Albert Nile
Major Religions	Protestantism, Roman Catholicism, Islam, native beliefs
Currency	(1,732.8 UGX = U.S. $1 as of July 2004)

Opposite: This painting is the work of Ugandan artist Nuwa Wamala Nnyanzi.

Glossary

ancestral: relating to family from the past, farther back than grandparents.

brotherhood: close friendship and good will between a group of people.

cassavas: plants with roots that can be cooked and eaten in many ways.

converts: people who have changed from one religion to another.

equator: an imaginary line around the exact middle of Earth.

ethnic: related to a race or a culture that has similar customs and languages.

fibers: long, thin strands taken from a material, such as banana leaves.

independent: related to being free from control by others.

legislative: relating to the law and the making of laws.

missionaries: religious people who go to another country to teach, spread their religion, and do good works.

native: belonging to a land or region by having first grown or been born there.

parliament: elected government group that makes the laws of their country.

plantains: a fruit similar to a banana.

plateau: a wide, flat area of land that is surrounded by lower land.

protectorate: a country that is protected and partially ruled by another country.

provinces: regions of a country with set borders and their own local officials.

Ramadan: the Islamic holy month. All healthy Muslims must not eat or drink until after dusk each day of the month.

rebel: relating to fighting against a ruler or government.

reserves: lands set aside so that animals and plants can survive there.

rural: related to the countryside.

sacrifices: offerings of valuable things, often an animal or person, to a god.

salvation: saving or being saved.

squash: a game in which players hit a hard rubber ball with a racket.

suburbs: towns or areas close to a city.

thatched: covered in natural materials such as straw or leaves to form a roof.

traditional: regarding customs or styles passed down through the generations.

urban: related to cities and large towns.

More Books to Read

Africa. Continents series. Mike Graf (Bridgestone Books)

Beatrice's Goat. Page McBrier (Atheneum)

Elephant Magic for Kids. Animal Magic for Kids series. (Gareth Stevens)

Good Morning, Gorillas. Magic Tree House series. Mary Pope Osborne (Random House Children's Books)

A Visit from the Leopard: Memories of a Ugandan Childhood. Catherine Mudibo Piwang, Edward Frascino (Pippin Press)

Wanyana and Matchmaker Frog: A Bagandan Legend. Legends of the World series. Melinda Lilly (Troll Communications)

Videos

Chimpanzees of Uganda. Champions of the Wild series. (National Film Board of Canada)

East Africa. Worlds Together for Kids series. (Worlds Together)

Travel the World by Train: Africa — Morocco, Tunisia, Egypt, Kenya, Uganda, South Africa. (Pioneer)

Uganda: The Pearl of Africa (Ambrose Video)

Uganda: Wildlife on the Edge. Investigative Reports series. (A&E Home Video)

Web Sites

kids.mapzones.com/world/uganda/

www.buganda.com

www.government.go.ug/

www.uwa.or.ug/index.html

Due to the dynamic nature of the Internet, some web sites stay current longer than others. To find additional web sites, use a reliable search engine with one or more of the following keywords to help you locate information about Uganda. Keywords: *amadinda, Idi Amin, Buganda, gorillas, Kampala, Lake Victoria, Obote, Victoria Nile.*

Index